Spirituality
in Business

The Hidden Success Factor

To ELAINE CAMPBELL

With best wishes for
the future

Mike Stephen

Spirituality in Business

The Hidden Success Factor

Michael Stephen

Chairman, Aetna International, Inc. (Retired)

Inspired Productions Press LLC
Scottsdale, Arizona

Spirituality in Business
The Hidden Success Factor

by Michael Stephen

Copyright © 2002 by Michael Stephen

Published by: Inspired Productions Press LLC
Scottsdale, Arizona

Cover design and layout by Ad Graphics, Inc., Tulsa, Oklahoma

Printed in the United States of America

ISBN: 0-9707140-2-5

Praise for

Spirituality in Business

The Hidden Success Factor

Mike Stephen is an international business leader who has walked his talk. When he says spirituality in business is the hidden success factor, you can count on it. He sure did and both his people and his company benefited greatly from his courage and vision in putting first things first. You will be inspired to reach inside and unleash your spirit at work.

John J. Scherer, author,
Work and the Human Spirit

I have been greatly impressed by the depth of Mike Stephen's appreciation of the diversity, as well as the commonality of human behavior in all aspects of social, political, economic and business life throughout the world. His vast experience is shared in this extremely well written book.

S. P. Hinduja, Chairman,
Hinduja Group of Companies

There are not many truly wise corporate leaders—so when one of them decides to share their heart and soul in the remarkable way Mike Stephen has, we would all be wise to read and re-read it. This conversational book is international in scope, intriguing in subject, and intimate in spirit. You will not find a better mentor.

Ian Percy, author,
Going Deep: Exploring
Spirituality in Life and Leadership

This is a delightful read. Mike has had a long and distinguished career, filled with strong personal relationships which are much deeper and richer than those normally found in today's business environment. His book explains why this is so.

Dominic D'Allessandro, President and CEO,
Manulife Financial

Mahatma Ghandi said, "My life is my message." Likewise for Mike Stephen his approach to life has been his formula for business success. A herald and harbinger of a New Age business leader, Mike shows in this fascinating account of his career as a senior insurance executive how spirituality can be a major factor in the success of a business enterprise. For CEO's who want to enrich not only their organizations but their souls, this book is a must read!

Stephen J. Solarz, President,
Solarz Associates

YES, you can be both Chairman of a major international insurance company *and* spiritual at the same time. Michael Stephen recounts, in endearing vignettes, how spirituality is both the foundation and the future of business. His book is warm, authentic and deeply spiritual— a must read for all current and future senior managers.

Martin Rutte, co-author,
Chicken Soup for the Soul at Work

This book highlights the importance of relationships, sensitivity to other's culture, spiritual leadership, and corporate culture. It is written in such simple language that one can easily identify with them. Michael's vast experience in Asia and Central and South America is clearly reflected in the way he analyses issues. His writing on the subject of spirituality in business, the need to form close personal relationships and a bond of trust with those with whom you deal in life are unique and mesmerizing. This is a book that spiritually takes you to a higher level of appreciation of those around you and underscores the importance of inner peace.

Dr. Mahathir bin Mohamad,
Prime Minister, Malaysia

Table of Contents

Foreword

This book is about my personal journey in business. Hopefully, this book will describe for the reader the positive impact of spirituality in business when it is enhanced, shared, and celebrated.

I am indebted to several business and political leaders in Asia and the Americas. They took the time and made the effort to help extend Aetna's presence in their countries without ever compromising their responsibilities to their companies or countries.

This work is a gift to my wife Bea, and our four children and their spouses: Christopher and Lisa, Michael and Linda, Joseph and Theresa and Andrea and Ron. In addition, it is a legacy to our grandchildren: Dominique, Michelle, Madeleine, Michael, Sarah and Erik.

Over a career that spans 40+ years, Bea and our children have been a source of strength, love and understanding.

Spirituality in life and in the workplace gives meaning and value to simple acts of kindness, friendship and understanding. In business it has, and continues to be, the hidden success factor so present in life.

Bea and I have been blessed and enriched with the privilege of sharing time and space with many friends and relatives on our journey.

In a special way I thank my editor, Susan Suffes, whose contribution was extraordinary and most helpful. Her competence and skill added a great deal to this message of spirituality in business. Her standards of excellence are admirable. Our friend and assistant, Lynn Hellinger, continues to provide order and the necessary competence to bring my thoughts and experiences on paper in a way that hopefully will inform the reader about a spiritual journey that is meaningful and ongoing.

My Spiritual Awakening

A defining moment occurred in my life in 1995 when I was invited to speak to a very diverse audience in Toronto on the subject of *Spirituality in the Workplace.* Even such a short time ago it was rather unusual for a businessperson to broach the subject of spirituality with others in the business world. In that speech I made my first public declaration that I had been actively meditating for 21 years.

Today the situation has changed somewhat since the partnering of business with spirituality is experiencing strong growth and increased popularity. A number of New Age leaders have grasped the necessity of personal transformation, which is realized when the spiritual side is acknowledged and nurtured. These insightful men and women know that when this happens, the company grows from within, making itself stronger and much more likely to profit.

Yet many other CEOs and business leaders are still reluctant to recognize the power that spirituality holds for them. In corporate America, there is concern that spirituality may be associated with a particular religion. Thus employees are expected to check their souls at the company gate.

I believe that it's time to throw open that gate and usher in a new business era. After all, major changes in organizational structures, employment contracts, and the whole notion of leadership have undergone enormous shifts and changes in the past decade.

Now, in a global marketplace, employees must feel connected to their corporations, their colleagues—no matter how foreign they may seem—and most of all to themselves. People respond more quickly when they feel there is a sincere interest in them as individuals. Without this spiritual link, success is not only comprised—it's undermined.

That's why leaders must set a precedent. Their conduct and style need to mirror their commitment to opening their companies to embrace the connection that binds all of us together. More than ever employees and all those with whom they do business, need to be understood, appreciated, recognized, and valued. As a result, loyalty and effectiveness will flourish. Only when spirituality is celebrated can this happen.

Many years ago in Toronto, a small group of Aetna employees participated in the Meals on Wheels program during their lunch hour. (Meals on Wheels is a volunteer service wherein hot meals are delivered to house-bound senior citizens.) When I learned of this venture, I asked if I might join them. The effect was dramatic because in those days it was rare to see a company president deliver a hot meal to an elderly person. This simple act helped create a more positive, not to mention spiritual, environment at the company. It communicated an important message about values, involvement, and generosity. The time I spent with employees involved in the project enriched our relationships.

More to the point, delivering the meals was personally rewarding for me. Our *clients* wanted us to stop in and visit; they were lonesome. At first I didn't realize that the person delivering the food was often the only contact the shut-in might have for days. When I went into home after home where the television was blaring, I suddenly realized that the television might be their only available company.

America must tap into its spiritual roots and make similar fundamental person-to-person connections if it is to continue as a world leader. In our global marketplace, companies are trans-national. That's why it is imperative to link with others— to embrace cultural and historical differences—in order to create new opportunities. I have learned, through decades in international business negotiations and agreements, that language and customs are not barriers to commercial success. On the contrary, there is a universal magnet, one constant, that draws us together to share time and ideas, and construct new and exciting prospects. That constant is the *spirituality* that we share with others. Once it is recognized it is able to transform and create an environment for success.

Building on this *spiritual* infrastructure, businesses can expand because their connections through the spirit can and will transcend any differences.

As companies expand internationally, there is a magnificent opportunity to positively impact those countries where North American companies operate. When you consider that half the world's population exists on less than two dollars a day, it's easy to imagine how changes could be implemented, both immediate and long-range. Part of the corporate mission could be to improve the economic life of workers. But unless, and until, the employer lives and works in an environment that honors and recognizes the spirit in everyone, this improvement may never happen.

Instead of looking outside at competitors for answers for growth and profitability, it can be more productive to look within ourselves to determine what the real global mission is.

Spiritual association is the surefire way to accomplish this. Starting person to person within a company and fanning out from there, the positive effect ripples out onto a worldwide pond.

The spiritual journey I've been on my entire life, encompassing my youth, my years in business, and my relationship with my family has brought me to this conclusion. God's spirit connects me to my neighbors, friends, and associates. It links me to the people with whom I work. It unites me in a special way to my wife Bea and our four children. And, of course, it bonds me to God.

Every CEO who seeks a permanent solution to corporate challenges by cost cutting and pulling tighter reins should realize there is another answer—a better answer. Spirituality is the critical aspect of our humanity that must be recognized because it assures success.

That is why spirituality in business *is* the hidden success factor.

CHAPTER ONE:

Finding My Place

Growing up in Saint John, New Brunswick, Canada, was not what I would call easy. My father, Louis, emigrated from Lebanon and married Eva, my mother. He was twenty-one; she was fifteen. They had twelve children: four girls and eight boys. I was their ninth. We were part of a group of fifty or so Lebanese Catholic families who settled in the Canadian province. My mother's parents were Lebanese as well, although she was born in Boston, Massachusetts.

As strangers in a strange land, we were treated as aliens for many years. Immigrants and their children were subjected to taunts and ridicule. Slowly over time this changed. By respecting differences and finding similarities in each other, the natives and newcomers eventually found a common ground. But it did take awhile.

In the meantime, my parents who owned a grocery store, and my grandmother who lived with us, established a model to live by. Their bright optimism and unwavering confidence reinforced the idea that life was good—especially when fifteen of us sat down at the dinner table. The words I remember hearing time after time were, "Don't worry. God will provide." And He did!

My father was one of the most positive individuals I've ever known. When his children complained and cried about being singled out and teased at school, my father dismissed our case by saying, "Don't worry; they don't mean it. They just don't know any better." His focus was to make sure that his children knew they were to succeed in life. Consequently, the desire to compete was instilled in each of us.

Outside the family he revealed another side of himself. Quietly, he extended help to those who were in need. He understood fully the tenet of being "his brother's keeper." Many years later at his funeral, several of our former neighbors spoke to my family about my father's many acts of kindness.

For me, one of the most pivotal events of my life occurred during my last year in high school. When Dad asked me how I ranked in the graduating class I responded, "I came in second."

"How come you didn't graduate first in your class?" he wanted to know.

Angry, I replied, "Dad, why don't you say this to your other children? How come you and I argue all the time?"

Pausing a moment, he looked at me and said, "Mike, you are different."

Thirty-four years later I understood what he was trying to tell me. That was the time he said, "Mike, don't you know that I love you?"

*   *   *   *   *

The seeds of my spiritual voyage were sown in those early years in Saint John. So convinced was I that a religious life awaited me that I gave long and serious thought to becoming a priest. By the third year of university I was convinced that I had chosen my vocation. In 1948, I entered the seminary where I spent the next three years preparing for ordination.

It was during that third year that doubts began to plague me. I worried and I prayed, but the reservations persisted. Finally, I made a fateful decision and left the seminary. In my wake, I left a terribly upset and disappointed family. As for me, I felt bitter and disillusioned. So many years spent in the seminary while my contemporaries were establishing themselves in their various careers, left me feeling betrayed. God, I believed, had not been good to me.

The question of what I was going to do with my life was answered when I remembered that as an undergraduate I had been a teaching assistant. "There's my career," I thought.

In my first full year as a teacher, I was assigned to a group of slow learners—teenagers with learning handicaps. I desperately wanted to help them, not because of any deep spiritual motivation but because they presented such a challenge. Apparently I achieved some success. Forty-four years later, after I received an honorary doctorate of letters from the University of New Brunswick, a middle-aged man walked up to me.

"I just want to thank you for making sure I could read " he said. When he mentioned his name, I remembered him as a member of that first class of mine so long ago. "I'm a very successful businessman today," he told me, "and I often think back to our days at Simonds Regional High."

I was blown away. This statement made more of an impact on me than the honorary degree. It took almost half a century for me to clearly see how the possibility of helping—or harming—is always present.

Looking back now, and putting it all into perspective, I realize how fortunate I was to have experienced where and how I grew up, and I am especially thankful for those seminary years. In many ways my religious training prepared me for teaching as well as the business world. Listening to others, paying attention to the voice of God as it came through me, and my own actions and reactions to others, were a proving ground that would serve me so well in the future.

Of course, I had a long way to go before I understood just how spirituality and business were intertwined.

CHAPTER TWO:

A New Way to Do Business

After a few years of teaching I stumbled into another career. A friend revealed to me what he was earning in the insurance business. Since it was so much more than I was earning as a teacher, I made a leap into something totally new. I had to do something because I wanted to marry Beatrice and an annual income of $2,500 was not enough to support a wife and the children we hoped for.

I joined London Life as a salesman in 1955 and I continued with the organization, working my way up until I was appointed branch manager in St. Laurent, Quebec.

While it may sound odd, the insurance business, which is seen by many as cold and uncaring, provided a platform to acknowledge the power of connecting with others. In those years the spiritual dimension of business took root for me. I saw that treating people the way I wished to be treated—with respect and understanding—was the way to build a career and live fully.

Even now after many years, I often think of my friend Rolland. He was a *superstar* salesman in our company until he was diagnosed with leukemia. But either because he couldn't accept the reality of the situation, or he wanted to hide it from his friends, he said he had thrown his hip out of joint. Visiting him regularly and pretending along with his adoring wife and daughter that his illness was temporary, was very painful for me. All of us played our part of the charade. Even when Rolland was weak and unable to walk, we acted as if all his debilitating symptoms would pass once his hip was better.

On most of my regular visits we talked little and yet we were present to each other, enjoying one another's company in the silence. At times he would drift off to sleep and then I would speak with his brave wife. The situation was heartbreaking. I had no medicine, no cure. All I could give to my friend was my presence before his passage to eternity.

Then there was the time when I was informed that one of my clients had been in a fatal accident. Going to the widow's home to complete the claims form was very difficult. When she recognized me at the door she immediately began to cry. I couldn't say a word but somehow we got the forms completed. She then reminded me of how resistant she and her husband had been to buying life insurance. She thanked me profusely for being quietly persistent.

I knew that the family would be able to carry on with dignity because the husband had bought life insurance. But

I saw beyond my salesman role and began to understand that I had a spiritual responsibility to my clients as well.

That moving experience gave new meaning to my life and work. It helped me understand that people everywhere have the same fears, needs, and wants.

A CHANGE INSIDE IS FELT OUTSIDE

Two major events happened in 1974: I joined Aetna in Toronto and I began to meditate.

Just before we left Montreal, a friend from university days who had experienced great personal turmoil gave me some invaluable advice. He said, "Mike, you should take up meditation. It's a way to listen rather than talk. You sit for about twenty minutes a day and quietly recite your mantra." Describing a mantra, he told me, "This *centering* will gradually give you peace and energy as you move into this new phase of your life. The quiet recitation of the mantra allows you to focus on the words. It centers the mind and reduces any distractions. Concentrating on the words of the mantra also relaxes the mind and the heart. What you experience is the silence and the peace of the moment. You listen to the silence. When distractions occur, returning to the mantra is the way to redirect the mind and soul to the interaction of the spirit in your space."

Intrigued, I began to meditate but it did not come easily to me. My progress was very slow but eventually I began to understand what my friend was talking about. The huge power of recognizing the existence of the spiritual dimension within my personal life, within the workplace, and among my family, friends, and associates became clearer. In the precious minutes of meditation it is possible to sense the personal spirit of God and know that you are loved and that your life has meaning.

Maranatha, Maranatha. This is the mantra that I recite silently every morning during my meditation. It is Aramaic, and translated it means, "Come Lord, Come Lord Jesus." Beyond the words, it invites the Lord to take up my heart and soul and show me His gentle direction for the day. It is a request to share the peace and joy of doing God's will for the next twenty-four hours as well as a plea to see His face in the wealthy as well as the destitute. It is a prayer that my life will be handed over to Him and that His spirituality will shine through my actions for that day.

However, reciting the mantra is not a simple process. Discipline and humility are necessary to allow God's spirit to work His infinite love. This is the work of a lifetime, one day at a time.

I remember attending a luncheon years ago with a couple of friends who were also daily meditators. One of them asked me if I was still meditating. "Yes," I replied, "but you know, after more than five years I still struggle with distractions from time to time."

"That's okay," he said. "The first ten or fifteen years are the toughest. After that it settles down."

He was right. Through meditation I saw how important it is to look for the good in people rather than what is bad, and to seek out and acknowledge what is right instead of what is wrong. This insight was instrumental in how I learned to interact with co-workers. The concept is simple: concentrate on a person's strengths rather than his or her weaknesses. It is a fundamental philosophy, yet too often it gets lost in office politics, policy memos, and trawling the bottom line for profits.

Meditation helped me to appeal to the heart as well as the intellect of those around me, no matter where I was or who I was with. As a spiritual resource, it replenished me every day.

When I arrived at Aetna, meditation played a great role in my success. It helped me to identify the critical and essential business issues I had to face and deal with them in a productive, and most of all, humane way.

THE EARLY AETNA YEARS

Before I went to Aetna I interviewed a number of senior executives there. In guarded language I heard that help was needed in a big way. One man when asked, "How bad is it?" replied, "Not bad. You can't fall off the floor."

At this time, Gordon Farquhar was President and CEO of Aetna Canada. Previously he had been a Vice President in Aetna's group division in Hartford, Connecticut, and his appointment marked the first time a person from the parent organization was sent from the U.S. Unfortunately, it was generally accepted that the Canadian organization was not meeting expectations. An outstanding person, Gordon was and is gentle, kind, and caring. We worked closely for over a dozen years and my admiration for him grew as the years passed. The reason was simple: he communicated his personal and sincere interest in the people with whom he worked. Not surprisingly, he boosted confidence in, and commitment from, his management team.

Hiring me to fix the individual life operation was one of his first executive decisions. Very low-key, he was persuasive and non-confrontational. His personality was ideal, given the reality that he was the first American sent in to fix the Canadian operation, which had been drifting under the previous regime.

Applying what I had already learned about acknowledging the spirit as well as the person, we began a new way of doing business. In short order, the staff began to respond with enthusiasm to the open, inclusive new environment.

Most people want to be part of a winning team. This important lesson was critical and in retrospect, quite obvious. The staff's renewal was deeply spiritual because of the give and take of trust and confidence demonstrated in equal proportion by everyone involved. The employees' response to the invitation to take responsibility and create change came from the heart. Accepting the expanded vision of their active roles, the men and women I worked with felt appreciated and valued. And because they did, so did I.

Doing work right, on time and every time, became the company's prime objective. Laughter and excitement were always present while we dealt with problems. Gradually, results improved and all of us were proud of our team's accomplishments. In this productive atmosphere, I was able to climb more corporate steps. In 1981, I was appointed Executive Vice President of Insurance Operations and in 1985, I was named President and Chief Operating Officer. Then in 1987, I succeeded Gordon Farquhar as President and CEO in Canada.

Throughout my time there spirituality guided me. Through daily meditation my role in management became less authoritative and more collaborative. *Doing* was more important than *saying*. Treating associates as partners and team members became a powerful, positive agent for change. Here is an example.

During my tenure as President, a catastrophic situation developed in the group claims department. A week after a new claims-paying system had been installed, it went down. Claims could not be paid and the employees were very upset. Their anger stemmed from a bigger source. It turned out that the *new, improved* system was designed without taking into account the very individuals whose responsibility it was to pay claims. How could the designers not consider an even more pertinent piece of information? In all of Aetna Canada the turnover rate was 12% a year—in the claims department it was 25%. Working in that division was an entry-level position; therefore, after paying their dues, employees moved on as soon as another opportunity presented itself.

To get to the root of the problem I asked the people in the claims department to a breakfast meeting. It was extremely interesting to say the least. At first there was a lot of cynicism—they had never before been invited to a breakfast meeting with a president and their defenses were up. A few were courageous enough to ask me if I knew how bad things were.

Then I asked them what they thought we should do. Basically, I asked for their help. They were shocked. When they recovered, many were openly critical of management who, they felt, would pay little attention to their views. Still, I prompted them to express their opinions about the new system.

They told me the system wasn't user-friendly; it was terribly complex and unnecessarily complicated. When I asked if they thought a new system should be installed or whether the existing one should be fixed they looked incredulous. They found it nothing short of amazing that their point of view should be taken into consideration.

At that meeting I suggested that we get together for a monthly breakfast throughout the next year as we reordered our priorities and dealt with this major business crisis. They readily agreed. When I asked what structure would best respond to the needs of the claim-paying function, their response was swift. They wanted to be organized into teams without supervisors, since they knew their work a whole lot better than their overseers did.

As soon as I agreed to their plan they quickly organized themselves and began working on redesigning a system that would function for users as well as clients. And, in spite of the technical problems, productivity began to improve. Intensely competitive, the teams would nonetheless assist one another with a particularly heavy workload.

The teams identified their objective: to pay every completed claim within five working days with a first-time accuracy of 92%. Their objective was met within one year.

I was so impressed by this accomplishment that I invited Ron Compton, then Aetna CEO in Hartford, Connecticut, to spend half an hour with our claims department. On his next Toronto visit he did—and he had to be dragged away after an hour and a half. He was elated by the enthusiasm as well as the competency of the staff. Their actions were clear reflections of the value they knew had been placed upon them.

Applying the lessons I learned from this success, I knew it was important to develop a company-wide *customer-services* strategy that would position Aetna Canada as the best in providing assistance.

Several seminars were held to teach this message and each proved to be a huge success. Employees acted like company ambassadors, proud to deliver outstanding customer service.

The project was so successful that it caught the eye of Gary Benanav, the President of Aetna International, Inc. (AII). The program was adopted and modified to fit the needs of particular countries. Then, in 1992, I was offered an opportunity I had not anticipated. Gary asked me if I could consider being a candidate to replace him. He had been promoted to Group Executive with expanded responsibilities. In 1994 he was promoted to Executive Vice-President.

I was 62 years old, and not anticipating a promotion. Gary assured me that he was aware of my age and suggested that there were still contributions I could make. I felt he was right, and later that year I was appointed President of Aetna International, Inc. The move to Hartford was going to take me on more of a spiritual journey than I had ever thought possible.

CHAPTER THREE:

Discovering a Universal Business Language

One of the most important tasks that I undertook as President of Aetna International, Inc., and later as Chairman, was to personally lead the discussions with potential joint-venture partners, regulators, and government leaders. I was involved in establishing joint ventures in Argentina, Brazil, Peru, Indonesia, and China. At the same time I was responsible for making sure that existing joint ventures in Malaysia, Hong Kong, Taiwan, Chile, Mexico, New Zealand, and Canada were nurtured.

Aetna's focus was to create new businesses in Central and South America and Asia. The economies in many countries in these areas were expanding by 8% to 10% yearly. In contrast, the economies of the U.S., Canada, and Europe were growing at a rate of 2% to 4% annually. In addition, the personal savings rate in many Asian countries was an astounding 25% to 30% annually, while in the U.S. it was about 1%.

My role put me into close contact with diverse groups of influential business leaders in the Americas and Asia. Sharing spiritual encounters with some of these fascinating individuals are among my most treasured recollections.

With each person I found a common ground, sometimes where I least expected one. Our shared belief system transcended politics or religion or profit. Time and again I saw a spiritual underpinning at work, which led my company and me to greater achievements. More importantly, it brought to me a more complete understanding of how all of us are connected.

THE MEXICAN CONNECTION

Don Eugenio Garza, who headed up the VAMSA Group, one of the largest conglomerates in Mexico, made a vivid impression on me. He spoke with great pride about his family. It was apparent that his role as husband and father superceded all other considerations and dominated his life. When he spoke, it was softly, with dignity. He asked many questions and, because of his style and demeanor, he created a very attractive, encouraging environment.

Don Eugenio was comfortable in allowing his business leaders a wide scope in crucial negotiations and he seldom attended the sessions. As we developed our joint venture with the VAMSA Group, it became obvious that they were tough negotiators. Still, every person was respectful, friendly, and forthright. They had no difficulty delineating the job of fashioning a workable joint venture along with the *relations building* that was so important to them. Once we all reached an agreement, they went to great lengths to make us feel comfortable. We were always welcomed as long-standing friends.

One of Don Eugenio's closest friends was Don Eduardo Elizondo, who was chairman of our joint venture. A particularly friendly and gracious man, his presence generated a familial and energizing spirit at board meetings. In even the most controversial discussions, he made sure that deference toward his partners—that included me and my team—was present. And it was genuine.

One time Don Eduardo described to me the impact of the 1996 devaluation of the Mexican peso on the Mexican middle class. With passion, he spoke about how young people had worked so hard to build a future. With emotion, he recounted the sense of deep disappointment and frustration that those men and women were experiencing. His concern and love for his fellow citizens were palpable.

Not surprisingly, the Mexican joint venture was a huge success because it was built on confidence and trust. It was expanded to include the pension business. Unfortunately, the worldwide recession of 1997 impacted severely on our partner's bank, and the joint venture came to an end with the sale of Aetna International to ING in 2000.

THE BRAZILIAN LINK

Like many U.S. companies, Aetna realized the advantages of a Brazilian operation as the economy there began to show promise. We had several discussions about forming a joint venture with a number of business groups in that country and, by some good fortune, we were directed to the Larragoiti family. They owned Sul America, the number-one insurance company in Brazil. Company leader, President and CEO Rony Lyrio, enjoyed the unqualified support of the owners.

The political decision to open up Brazilian domestic markets to foreign competition was poised to bring about vast changes. Sensing what was about to take place, the Larragoiti family began a search for an international partner. The family understood that the experience and level of competency that had worked in a *closed* domestic market would not survive very well in an open market. A foreign partner could bring new techniques and effective competition to the mix.

I spent a great deal of time building a personal relationship both with Rony and Patrick Larragioti, the Chairman of Sul America. After months of dialogue, Rony said to me, "We like you and your people. They're great; they're different. They don't tell us what to do and how they can help us. You pay much more attention to the building of confidence for our potential joint venture. This approach makes me feel more comfortable."

I'm convinced that we were selected because of our mutual objective to build a joint venture based on partnership and respect. Great attention to the spiritual aspect of the union—rather than presenting a brag sheet of accomplishments—seemed more appealing to everyone involved. It was shortly after this discussion that we were informed that Aetna was the selected partner.

Soon after that, Rony arranged for us to meet H.E. Fernando Henrique Cardoso, the President of Brazil. President Cardoso greeted us warmly in his magnificently furnished office outside of Rio de Janeiro. He asked thoughtful questions and spoke at great length about the need for Brazil to prepare for the on-rushing global market place. He stressed that it was important for his country to compete effectively in that arena in order to improve economic life there.

With a real show of humility that was genuinely moving, he said, "Thank you for coming to Brazil to help us build a future together." This was a first for me. I had never before witnessed the president of a country taking the time to thank Aetna for entering its borders. This gentleman's life as a politician, a refugee, a university professor, and an exile from Chile had, I believe, made a profound effect on his life and added to his insight and wisdom. His experiences molded a compassionate human being whose every word and gesture resonated with spirituality.

THE CHILEAN CONNECTION

I first met Sergio Baeza when he joined Aetna to head up its fledgling business in Chile. An international businessman, he spoke fluent French and English as well as his native

Spanish. Under his leadership, revenues and earnings grew at exceptional rates. Wisely, he surrounded himself with a very competent group of senior managers who shared his vision to have Aetna Chile recognized as the number one insurance group in his country. His success was so well known that his operations became the model copied by his competitors.

Not surprisingly, a powerful family known as the Lusic Group developed a keen interest in buying part, or even all, of the Chilean operation. Repeatedly they tried to entice Sergio to support their effort but for several reasons Sergio did not find them a good fit. In the meantime, the Vice Chairman of Aetna, Dick Huber, was approached by Lusic to support their goal. Dick informed me that we should seriously consider their offer. When told of this development, Sergio was terribly shaken and thought that I was against him.

Finally I went to speak with Dick to review the situation fully and understand the consequences of selling a percentage of the Chilean operation to the Lusic Group. I told him that if we went ahead we would receive Sergio's resignation personally within 24 hours.

"I don't believe it," he exclaimed.

"You better be prepared," I replied. "There is only one way to find out."

Dick decided not to press the issue.

To this day, Sergio (now Chairman of Aetna, S.A.) and I still maintain our relationship although we have little face-to-face contact. He is like a son to me. A believer in strong personal relations with his people, he is a deeply religious man. He honors his family, his business associates, and all of those with whom he conducts business.

*   *   *   *   *

The business leaders in Central and South America impressed me with their spiritual roots, which seemed to direct and focus their vision on the cultural and human dimension of their businesses. Yes, they expected solid financial performance—but in a way that preserved human dignity along with a high level of focused mission.

This spirit-based business model seemed be the springboard for effective leadership in both private and public life. Their standard was one I would yet witness and be profoundly touched by, on other continents as well.

CHAPTER FOUR:

The Power of Spirit in China

China presented new challenges and alliances. Although the cultures of our countries differed greatly, there was one unifying factor that determined success. Whenever there was a spiritual underpinning to the proceedings, a deeper more profound association took place. That bond transcended business and served to link us. With that tie, accomplishments on many levels inevitably followed.

THE CHINA CONNECTION

As Aetna strove to gain a license in China, I was fortunate to meet influential political leaders whose spirituality guided their decisions. Li Dayou, the Chinese Ambassador to the U.S. from April, 1993, to March, 1998, was part of this special group.

One of the most interesting and insightful individuals I have had the good fortune to encounter, the Ambassador's behavior was symbolic of the spiritual underpinnings of his country. I first met him in Washington, D.C., because Aetna wanted to inform him of its commitment and plans to secure a license in China. Additionally, I wanted to ask his advice about what should and should not be done to make that happen.

Extremely discreet and guarded, he made no promise but made an effort to understand our position. And he certainly seemed pleased that the team observed proper protocol by informing him of our intentions and requesting his support. Before each visit to China, I made it a point to inform Ambassador Dayou of our game plan and request particular recommendations and advice from him.

Eventually, the Ambassador became our advocate in Beijing and his support helped Aetna in its quest for a license. On a personal level, I became friends with him and we had lunch in New York prior to the end of his term of duty. A short time after his wife died, I expressed sorrow in person on behalf of Aetna. He was genuinely touched. At the farewell lunch he talked about how much he missed his wife and nodded when I said, "Ambassador Li, I'm sure that your good wife is with God and at peace."

When I retired from Aetna he wrote me a warm, memorable letter. It reflected a friendship filled with spirit. I am lucky to know him.

THE CHINESE WAY

AIG (American International Group) was the first foreign company awarded an insurance license in China. Aetna was also in pursuit of a license, and our reasoning was that we should be the second company to be selected.

The Aetna interpreter was a man named Ka Ning. A good teacher as well as a marvelous translator, his ability and expertise frequently saved the day. I believe that a life-changing event contributed to his skills. Several years ago, he injured his leg so badly that he thought it would have to be amputated. His surgeon examined his leg for a long time and then said, "Ka Ning, with my skill and God's help we are going to save your leg."

The combination worked, and Ka Ning began his spiritual journey. A person whose life and work ethic are exemplary, he was very effective in building important relationships. His talents contributed to our eventual success in a very big way.

Through the hard work of Ka Ning and our consultant, we were accorded a meeting with Premier Zhu Rongji. This happened after very careful nurturing of our relationship with the Chinese bureaucracy and the involvement of Ambassador Li Dayou in Washington, D.C.

During the meeting, there was an unexpected turn. The Premier asked how we planned to submit our application. Everyone turned to Doug Henck, the Hong Kong resident vice president, for a reply. Eloquent and more than a little evasive, he literally danced around the question and suddenly ended his response with these words: "Obviously, Mr. Premier, we would be influenced by any counsel or direction you might provide." At that point the Premier suggested that perhaps forming the joint venture with a Chinese company might go well with the decision-makers.

Asking for advice and assistance are powerfully persuasive components. Building a relationship with no conditions attached is essential in order to be accepted and appreciated. It's a very spiritual way of doing things.

Subsequently, I learned that China Pacific Insurance Company (CPIC) was going to be our partner if and when we were granted a license. Chairman Pan Q. Chang, who was President of China Pacific, was very gentle and almost deferential. Friendly and gracious, he emphasized repeatedly how much Aetna was doing for the joint venture.

The approval involved the most senior decision-makers in Beijing and, while Chairman Pan assured me of CPIC's support, it was up to us to convince the authorities that we were the right partner for them. Eventually, three letters of intent were signed with Chairman Pan stating our desire to form a joint venture partnership in the greater Shanghai area.

During one of our meetings he asked if I could remain for a few minutes after the session was concluded. After the others left, he said that there was a personal request he would like me to consider. He added quickly that if I could not respond favorably to the appeal he would understand. His daughter, Don-Jin, and son-in-law George, he explained, were completing their post-graduate studies in the United States. Don-Jin was studying finance, while her husband's area was systems development. He wondered if I might help them find work for two or three years. After that period of time they would return to Shanghai.

I promised that I would do what I could. With their impressive skills it wouldn't be hard to secure them positions at Aetna in Hartford. Then Chairman Pan asked a very special favor. He asked if I would be their *uncle* while they were in the United States. At first I didn't fully understand just what this meant but soon it became clear: I would act as a surrogate parent in place of Chairman Pan. This was an extraordinary compliment and responsibility.

I realized that this request was another indication of the growing relationship that had developed over time. My role as uncle meant that I would represent Chairman Pan if and when any personal or business crisis developed. I realized that I was being accorded a title of honor as a senior family friend.

At the same time I wasn't particularly concerned about any business risks growing out of this request. In Asia there is little division between the business and personal side of one's life, unlike the Western world where they are usually kept separate.

In a career that spanned more than fifty years, I had never been asked by either a Canadian or an American to be an uncle to their offspring. Yet here was a *stranger* who intensified his business relationship in a positive way. He gave me a huge vote of confidence by making a personal request for assistance in a private matter. Because of his special appeal, a friendship developed between two men who shared common attributes of love and family concerns.

On later visits to Shanghai, I would remain after our meetings and fill Chairman Pan in on his family. While in the U.S., Don-Jin had given birth to a son and yet another development occurred. Don-Jin and George, who I saw once a month for lunch, informed me that they wanted to remain in the U.S. for the foreseeable future and return to Shanghai at a later date—later than the two or three years they had initially thought. When I asked Don-Jin if she had informed her father about their decision her answer took me by surprise.

"No," she answered timidly. Then she added, "We wondered if you could talk with him." Don-Jin effectively called on her uncle to deliver the message to her father. When I spoke about this surprise and how disappointed her father would be, she remained silent and respectful. It was obvious that the decision of trust was final.

On my next visit with Chairman Pan I informed him that I carried a rather difficult message and proceeded to tell him about the decision that Don-Jin and George had made. I was more than a bit nervous. After all, not only was I the messenger bearing distressing news, I was the designated uncle.

Once he absorbed the disquieting news his eyes filled with tears. Understanding his pain, I continued. "Chairman Pan, I am a father and grandfather and I, too, have children who do not live in our country. I know how you feel."

There was a long silence. Then he reached out and touched my arm gently and said, "Chairman Stephen, please continue to be their uncle."

I did so, gladly.

* * * * *

In 2000, Chairman Pan attended a meeting in Washington, D.C., and then traveled to Hartford and invited me to a dinner celebration. He was overjoyed. His daughter, son-in-law, and grandson were going to return to China. Tenderness and joy marked the occasion and I was once again moved by the trust this man had put in me. Our relationship was a big link in the China connection.

My next lesson was to learn patience. Working diligently to secure license approval, I traveled to China over a dozen times. During those visits, I met with Vice Minister Sun Zhenyu of MOFTEC (the Ministry of Foreign Trade and Economic Cooperation) about as many times.

On one of those occasions I was particularly disappointed because China had just awarded a license to a European company. My feelings spilled over into my demeanor and with irritation in my voice I spoke about the length of time Aetna had devoted to securing a license, as well as trying to act like good corporate citizens.

During my tirade, Vice Minister Sun nodded gently and paid attention to what I was saying. When I was done, he looked at me intently and said, "Chairman Stephen, you're right. You've been coming to China for a long time. The leadership of the country appreciates that and you've made many friends. You've made contributions to the country and your experience and knowledge will help China. We believe that Aetna will make a valuable contribution to the life insurance business once it is doing business here. But you know this is China and one needs to be patient."

I felt so frustrated, but relating my frustration would, I knew, be extremely ill mannered in front of our hosts and produce nothing of value. Instead I said, "Vice Minister Sun, you are so right. I've learned much from my visits to your country. I've met good friends, like you. I've had the opportunity to fully understand China's rich culture and its history. I've been able to see the dynamic changes going on in the country and the market place. I'm deeply grateful for all of the lessons I'm learning, especially the lesson of patience. I started coming to China when I was a young man with black hair like yours. Now look at me. I'm old and gray."

With that, the Minister burst out laughing, as did all his team. My message got across in a way that was acceptable and totally understandable. I know from my experiences in China that poking fun at yourself is an effective way to communicate important messages. So why not take the heat in front of the Vice Minister in a way that would assure his support for our efforts?

Soon after this meeting, word began circulating that Aetna would shortly be granted a license. When I went to pay my respects to Chairman Jiang Mianheng, President Jiang Zemin's son, I knew right away that we had won. As he entered the room he greeted me with glee. "Chairman Stephen," he asked, "is your hair turning black?"

All the hard work and honesty that the team put in paid off the next year, 1997, when it was announced that Aetna was the second American company to secure approval for a license in China.

Within a few months of our license approval, there was a restructuring of several important ministries. These changes were made in anticipation of China's entry into the World Trade Organization (W.T.O.) and designed to shift the responsibility for the economy from the state to the individual. The Ministry of Labor and Social Security was created to implement this major decision. Zhang Zouji was chosen as minister, and our team was the first foreign business group that he agreed to meet.

As soon as the meeting began it became clear that the minister was outgoing and friendly. When I told him that we were deeply appreciative of his time since he had so many pressing obligations, his answer revealed his integrity. He replied that is was true that he was busy, but that he always had time for friends who might help him and his responsibilities. The meeting was a big success—just how big a success was revealed to me a couple of months later.

At that time, Minister Zhang was in Washington, D.C., leading a visiting delegation. At a dinner, which I hosted for him, we continued our discussions. In response to my request to play a role in pension privatization, Minister Zhang replied, "Aetna will be the first company permitted to sell pension products once the market is open to private companies."

This was a significant breakthrough. I seldom if ever heard this type of commitment from either the political or the economic leadership in China. The power of friendship and trust had prevailed.

Once again, the force of spirituality at work helped us succeed. By centering on challenges rather than on our own fragile egos we won the confidence of the Chinese. Establishing friendly relations was more important than attempting to prove how great we were and what terrific products we could sell. Ka Ning said it best: "The Chinese like you and they trust us."

I feel that the connections made had less to do with dollars and cents and much more to do with creating an atmosphere for growth and possibility and friendship. Indeed, the Vice Minister still considers me part of his extended American family, just as I consider him part of my wide-ranging Chinese family. This kind of alliance can only be formed when the spirit guides us to do what is right.

THE SPIRIT REVEALS ITSELF IN MANY WAYS

As we went about building relations with the regulators and government people, we had the good fortune to be introduced to Dr. Zhang Xiang and soon established a warm relationship with him.

In addition to his other duties, Dr. Zhang was Dean of the Business School at Shanghai Jiao Tong University. Among the first Chinese scholars permitted to travel to the United States to continue his post-graduate education, he received his Ph.D. from Columbia University. Both publicly and privately he stated that in his view, China needed America's expertise and know-how. He also believed that China needed Aetna's insurance expertise as the country was opening up to the insurance industry. A number of administrators based in China had told us the same thing.

As a declaration of good will, a long-term commitment was necessary. It turned out that the Chinese wanted Aetna to build a business school in Jiao Tong and assist in the curriculum development to meet international standards. Aetna had already conducted many seminars and training programs with particular emphasis on actuarial and legal issues and we were pleased to make the commitment before the approval of our license.

Dr. Zhang, with strong support from Dr. Sam Yin, our partner in Taiwan, convinced us to make that commitment. Dr. Zhang later became a Vice Minister of MOFTEC. Prior to the important promotion he spent approximately 18 months in the U.S. at the Chinese Council General's office. We visited frequently either in Hartford or New York. His guidance and counsel were enormously helpful.

In turn, Dr. Zhang introduced us to Dr. Xie Shengwu, the President of Shanghai Jiao Tong University (SJTU), as well as the Chairman of the Board of Governors. Meanwhile within our own company, we pondered how the Aetna School of Management would be defined. There was a strong desire to assure that over time the school would be recognized as a world-class institution. As we pondered the curriculum and faculty, this intention was always foremost.

I remember exchanging this view with President Xie and the business faculty at one of our board meetings. As our discussions became more enthusiastic, I got so carried away that I said, "President Xie, I would like to think that by the time my grandchildren are old enough to attend post-graduate school, they may want to consider the business school of SJTU."

In response, President Xie smiled. I knew I had touched a very emotional cord and that he was enormously complimented by this possibility.

In April, 2000, the Aetna Business School at Jiao Tong was officially opened. The day before the opening ceremony, President Xie and I paid our respects to Xu Kuangdi, the Mayor of Shanghai. President Xie echoed my sentiments about my grandchildren attending the school. Mayor Xu replied that if that ever were the case he would assure that my grandchild would receive a scholarship from the city.

The day of the opening ceremony I mentioned Mayor Xu's generous offer and added that, though I wasn't sure of this, I presumed that President Xie would approve admittance for my grandchild, "even if his or her marks weren't as good as they ought to be."

The audience began clapping and laughing because I was talking about family and dreams and hopes that we all shared. Summing up my thoughts, I said, "We came to China ten years ago as strangers. We became friends after a few years. Today we are family."

Then President Xie spoke eloquently of his personal dreams for the business school and his hope that the cooperative involvement he had experienced with Aetna's team would continue for many years into the future. Then he paused and said, "In appreciation for Chairman Stephen's leadership and personal involvement, the university has named its library the Michael Stephen Library."

This was an unexpected and touching result of spiritually-based exchanges in all their simple power.

WE'RE NOT AS DIFFERENT AS WE THINK

One of the surprises I experienced in working with the Chinese was to understand that they had the same needs for respect and acceptance as any of us from the West.

When we met with Jiang Zemin, the President of China, he said that the discussions about differences and politics as well as economic growth reminded him of an obscure Chinese poem. In translation, I heard the enlightening words, "Though we are separated by politics and thousands of miles, we share the same light of the moon."

In China I witnessed countless acts of generosity, kindness, and sensitivity. While my friends in China do not use the term *God*, they acknowledge a power greater than what is seen with the eyes. Spirituality exists in Communist China. When it is tapped, good things flow.

CHAPTER FIVE:

Profitable Discoveries from Painful Detours

Aetna's business also took me to other parts of Asia including India, Malaysia, and Indonesia. My experiences there were rich and textured.

My India experience was bolstered dramatically by Steve Solarz, President of Solarz Associates, an international consulting firm. He was, in addition, a Senior Counselor at APCO Associates, a Washington, D.C, public affairs firm. For twenty-four years, Steve had served in public office in both the New York State Assembly and in the U.S. House of Representatives. As a congressman, he had traveled widely and had met with dozens of world leaders, emerging as a leading spokesman on behalf of democracy and world rights.

Acting as a consultant on India to Aetna, Steve served as a kind of guide for me, introducing me to Indian business and political leaders as well as the essence of the country. The first time I went to New Delhi in Steve's company, I was totally unprepared for the overwhelming poverty that pressed against our car. The first time the car stopped at a traffic light, our windows were tapped and we could see people with outstretched palms. The country manager who accompanied us said, "They're begging and there are lots of them. Just keep your eyes ahead."

"I can't do it," I said. "I'm not doing this for them. I'm doing it for me." Steve understood what I meant and started fumbling for change too. Even if I was being conned, I was still emotionally distraught at the distress of the supplicants. I rolled down my window and Steve and I handed out all the ten-rupee notes we carried. It seemed like so little; after all, ten rupees was worth about twenty-five U.S. cents. But at least that sum would purchase a modest meal. Later, the country manager commented that he understood my reaction and wanted me to know that when he was alone he often gave the beggars money. The accepted rule was to *pretend* the beggars were not there!

Through meditation I learned that I must be my brothers' keeper and I made it a habit not to pass by a street person without giving some money. I realized that I could be seeing the face of God in that beggar.

One morning, a woman with a baby pleaded with us for money. On this particular day I had forgotten to get smaller notes at the hotel and discovered I carried only a hundred-rupee note. I hesitated for a moment and then handed her the money. Gasping at her good fortune the woman quickly disappeared into the teeming crowd. The next day the same woman was waiting for us. She smiled and waved but did not approach the car. She just wanted to greet me and wish me a good day. I had become her friend, not her mark. My faith in humanity was reaffirmed.

This reaffirmation continued when I met influential and powerful people as I sought to secure an acceptable Indian partner for our joint venture once the government opened the market for foreign competition. To move the process along, Steve introduced me to a number of people. All of them welcomed him as a family member. There was a genuine feeling of respect and intimacy that was obvious as Steve spoke about the purpose of our visit. It was very easy to get caught up in the warmth and generosity of spirit no matter who he introduced me to, including government officials.

One of the most impressive was Chief Minister N. Chandrababu Naidu, who came from the state of Andhra Pradesh. He spoke eloquently about the goal of his state to become an information technology capital of Asia. The Chief Minister spoke with reverence when he described how his state would then be able to look after the needs of its citizens. It was no surprise to me when I learned recently that Microsoft had chosen Hyberabad, the capital of the Minister's state, as a development center for technology outside of the United States.

Steve also introduced me to the President of India, K.R. Narayanan. The Aetna team met him after we requested a brief meeting as a matter of protocol, as well as to express our interest in entering the insurance market. Attentive and smiling, he listened closely to our purpose and intent. He, too, seemed to radiate with the spiritual essence so prevalent in India. It was a marvelous experience.

Meeting with Sonia Gandhi, the daughter-in-law of the late Prime Minister, Indira Gandhi, was notable as well. Sonia had experienced a double blow: both her husband, Rajiv (who was also Prime Minister), and her mother-in-law (Rajiv's mother) were assassinated. Yet Sonia continues in politics as the leader of the opposition party in Parliament. I believe her sense of obligation to her fellow citizens, as well as to her family and what they stood for, drives her on.

Another memorable businessperson was S.P. Hinduja, Chairman of the Hinduja Group of Companies. Friendly and open, S.P. asked me my age during our first meeting. Seventy, I told him. Jokingly, he replied, "No, you are thirty. You see, in India we think of life in terms of one hundred years, thus you have thirty more years and that is your age."

I discovered that the great wealth and power of the Hinduja Group is mirrored in their generosity. Making large contributions to a number of worthwhile charities around the world is part of their operation. The Hinduja Group focuses on providing health and education of a world-class standard, free of charge to those who cannot afford them, exemplified by the standards of the Hinduja National Hospital in Mumbai. It is clear to me that these displays of kindness are performed not for any special reward or recognition but because they are the right things to do.

Perhaps not so surprisingly I discovered that S.P. meditates for an hour a day. When he speaks of spirituality and its power, he does so in very simple terms. He understands that inner peace is a requisite for lasting success. That serenity supports his soul and provides inner strength as he deals with a myriad of global issues.

Mr. N. Rangachary, appointed Chairman of the Insurance Regulatory Authority, also made a profound impact on me. I first met him in Hartford where he came to observe Aetna's operations first-hand. Abhaya Jain, our India country manager, arranged the meeting. It turned out that the Chairman had worked for Abhaya's father at one point in his career. The relationship that was established was passed on from father to son. This fascinated me because in our western culture personal relations are much more short-term. In this case, confidence, trust, and reliance were already in place. Perhaps the Chairman's tranquil demeanor rose from this circumstance. I could not recall this kind of connective experience when I met with Western political leaders. This is less a criticism than an enigma. Perhaps Asian leaders regard their stewardship role in a different way. My sense is that Asians possess a better fix on their place in history because their cultures date back thousands of years. They seem to understand that whatever power they exercise—no matter how few or many years it is—is just a second in the course of their history. Because they understand that their time in power will pass and they will continue to live through their children and grandchildren, family is central to their being.

I found that the Chairman's spirituality shone through every gesture. Attentive and smiling, he nodded as our purpose and intent was described to him. Like many of the leaders of his country, he seemed to radiate the spiritual pulse of India.

Although Aetna never did receive a license to function in India, I found that many wonderfully spiritual connections existed with all kinds of people. When I think about my time there I know it was well spent.

THE MALAYSIAN CONNECTION

In 1997, Aetna needed help in Malaysia. Our partner, AUI (Aetna Universal Insurance), wanted to reduce the ownership position within our joint venture. Aetna had been permitted to buy up to 80% of AUI in 1991 on the condition that within seven years we would sell down our ownership to 49%. This was the maximum amount that a foreign insurer could own. By 1997, we wanted to retain our majority position.

However, Bank Negara, which regulated the life insurance industry, allowed Aetna to hold its position. It was understood that within five years we would sell the shares that gave us a majority. By this time, the deadline was approaching and we wanted to hold onto those deciding shares indefinitely. To make this happen both the bank and the Prime Minister,

Y.A.B. Data Seri Dr. Mahathir bin Mohamad, the Prime Minister, had to hear our appeals.

After interviewing a number of consultants who could assist Aetna's effort in Malaysia, we chose Kate Clemans. I was impressed with Kate the first time we met. Very outgoing, she didn't take herself seriously, while at the same time an aura of kindness and openness surrounded her. She could be extremely demanding where business was concerned, but she was very sensitive to people issues as well.

With her impressive knowledge of the regulatory environment, Kate recommended that I meet with Dr. Mahathir at the APEC (Asia Pacific Economic Cooperation) conference being held in Vancouver that year. Well known to the Prime Minister (Kate had lived in Malaysia for many years with her first husband), she was able to arrange the meeting. Before the meeting began she told me that the Prime Minister was a devout Moslem and a very spiritual person. He prayed, fasted dutifully, and traveled to Mecca even though his health was anything but robust. The meeting went well and I found the Prime Minister to be an engaging, friendly person although somewhat shy.

Within a month of that engagement I flew to Kuala Lumpur with Kate to present a detailed explanation of our position to Dr. Mahathir. As we traveled, Kate filled me in about timing and the political context in which Malaysian business decisions were made. In many ways she helped me understand the paradox of the Prime Minister, how his public persona differed from the person I met privately. Committed to leading his country to first-world status, his vision occasionally provoked emotional outbursts at those forces he perceived as trying to keep his nation and its people from their rightful place in the sun. Reserved and reflective, he was extremely concerned for the poor in Asia. At the same time he was passionate in his criticism of the West and its unbridled capitalistic system, which he contended forced the third world countries to be exploited in the extreme.

At the meeting with the Prime Minister we presented our position and asked for a postponement of selling down our shares. We were convinced that asking for a postponement was more acceptable to the Prime Minister and his government than asking for a change of law. Several meetings with various government officials were also held and respects to the Prime Minister were paid every time we visited his country.

Finally, a letter arrived from Bank Negara that extended the sell down requirement for another five years. It was a major victory and one that was attained because we worked within the framework of the country. We found a way that suited both our needs.

In 1999, I was elected Vice Chairman of the Malaysian U.S. Business Committee. At this point our Malaysian management were in discussions with the tax department in Kuala Lumpur, a dialogue that continued for several months. Our people did not handle these discussions effectively. Egos were ruffled within the government when it seemed that Aetna was trying to show the Malaysian bureaucrats the errors in their position. Things took a turn for the worse when the Minister of Finance didn't mince any words and spoke to me harshly in public. He accused Aetna of trying to put something over on the Malaysians.

Recognizing the vast cultural differences between Westerners and Asians, I outlined a long, carefully worded letter of apology to the Finance Minister. In this letter I asked for the opportunity for him to once again review our position.

It worked. The minister's deputy agreed to meet with us in Washington, D.C, and there we came to terms that suited us both. As a result, the relationship between Aetna and the Malaysian government was strengthened to the point where the Prime Minister asked me, as Chairman of the MUSBC (Malaysia U.S. Business Committee), if the group could help improve the tourist trade. Despite the fact that Malaysia was filled with wonderful people and blessed with excellent weather and much beauty, American travelers had little motivation or encouragement to visit the country.

Sensing a priceless chance to build on our existing relationship, we promised the Prime Minister that a game plan would be developed that he could review on his next trip to the States three months hence. At that meeting, several representatives from the travel business, including American Express and Starwood Hotels, were present. Both accepted very important leadership roles in concert with the Malaysian

Ministry of Tourism. From that point, a strategy was worked out and implemented and today there are high expectations that it will be successful.

The entire Malaysian project intensified my spirituality and reliance on God to lead. Kate and I would often attend mass at the local Catholic Church near the Shangri-La Hotel in Kuala Lumpur. It was always uplifting to see the number of young families attending services there. It spoke well of the political leadership, where Christians and Moslems could worship freely without fear. Dr. Mahathir constantly alluded to the fact that there was religious freedom in his country.

This expression of spirituality flowed from the Prime Minister. I feel that Aetna's achievements in Malaysia were due to his sense of ease with me because I tried to understand what was important to him. Without this spiritual connection that inspired trust and confidence, there would have been no success.

THE INDONESIAN CONNECTION

Usman Admadjaja, the Chairman of the Bank of Danamon, was another example of a spiritual leader. An intriguing person, Chairman Usman was from modest means and he used his drive and abilities to accumulate substantial wealth and power. Nonetheless, I always found him to be modest and grateful about his enormous success. There were many opportunities for me to see this because Aetna and the Danamon Bank held many discussions to determine whether to form a joint venture. From our point of view, the reasons were sound. The bank was not only the sixth largest in Indonesia, it had also embarked on an aggressive growth strategy. Eventually that joint venture became a reality, aided in no small way by the behavior of the Chairman.

I found him to be fair and open-minded in even the most difficult of circumstances, including the worst bank failures (the result of an extreme Asian financial crisis), that Indonesia had ever experienced.

When tempers flared and conversations became heated, Chairman Usman was consistently gracious and sensitive. He always took into consideration each person's opinion and feelings.

This spiritual stance helped all of us survive a financial crisis. His profound connection to forces greater than what was said, led to the solution of problems. He helped us solve our predicaments through a strong sense of obligation to do what was right.

Our problems with the joint venture were settled before the crisis brought down the bank. Chairman Usman, trying to find a viable middle ground that we all could live with, suggested *sharing* our businesses. We agreed to allow them to sell back 25% of Danamon Aetna to us. They agreed to sell us 25% of the Bank Assurance subsidiary. Thus we were 75%-25% of one company and 25%-75% of the other. In this way we could continue to be partners in the market.

Sadly, the venture didn't work because the bank failed. Yet this was another example of how one man, in an effort to make a difference, sought to find the solution where everyone would profit.

Once again I was given the chance to see how powerful the spirit is, especially in difficult times. Unfortunately, as time went on, I was not going to find the same situation at Aetna.

Chapter Six:

Spiritual Whiplash on the Aetna Roller Coaster

From the mid-1970s until 1996, spirituality had a consistent presence at Aetna. Filled with a sense of family and community, many individuals, including CEOs, extended their commitment to making life better outside the office. These generous people helped the disadvantaged in Hartford as well as other areas of the country. In fact, reaching out into the community was part of Aetna's culture. At the same time, Aetna employees enjoyed excellent benefits.

A high degree of spirituality was exhibited by Dr. Gerry Ross, currently the dean of the business school at McGill University in Montreal, and his associate, Michael Kay, who were brought into our Canadian organization as consultants. Their insightful and visionary suggestion—to make each of our career managers into independent, self-employed entrepreneurs—had a strong spiritual component to it. Both men spoke with integrity and honor, showing great patience with and respect of those who did not agree with them. By doing so they were able to persuade people to buy into a new concept of business in a way that let all participants feel like winners.

Convincing twenty-five senior branch managers that they would be better off accepting new arrangements in which they would be responsible for expenses including electricity, heat, rent, staff and salaries was a big challenge. Compensation would be performance-based. Yet, because the managers trusted the people who presented the plan, they accepted the new proposition and never looked back.

To this day the branch managers—and not one left when the new plan was proposed—admit that the change was for the better. Being in charge of their own destinies rather than relying on the organization to take care of them, has made these people much more productive and confident.

During those years several spiritually-motivated speakers were also brought to Aetna to either consult with CEOs or address groups of managers. These men made a significant impact on me. Each in his own way helped me more fully understand and appreciate the profound effect of spirituality in business.

Dr. Paul Rubyni was the first one of these influential people. Referred to me by a friend, he taught me that organizations, like people, have a body and a soul. He called this the spirit of the organization. "Not to recognize this,"

Paul told me, "is to court ultimate failure and disaster." He spoke about an organization as a distinct, living being, and compared organizational behavior with individual personal behavior.

According to Paul, good morale was the primary responsibility of the CEO who, after all, maintained the power and authority to change the organization and its employees. He told me that CEOs held the responsibility to lead and to breathe spirit into their organizations, and must do so if that organization was to survive and prosper. He helped me understand how important a role spirituality could play if a CEO understood its significance. He also convinced me that failed leadership leads to failed business.

Another influential speaker was Ian Percy, whom I introduced to the Aetna organization in Canada and the U.S. He consistently displayed his ability to blend depth of insight with a very effective use of humor. Ian took his first degree in theology and education but, despite the many ministers and missionaries in his family, he never felt that the pulpit was the way for him to reach out to the world. Instead, his sense of calling has taken him to the global corporate arena and his message is one that calls on leaders to bring meaning to the workplace. To do that, he exposes the biases and preconceived notions of leadership and team building.

According to Ian, senior officers need to feel good about themselves. They must be at peace and feel humble enough to ask for help. He also believes that CEOs should recognize that employees are put in their care by a higher power and that the creation of an environment where employees can do their best work—that is perform with a clear sense of meaning and purpose—is the CEO's responsibility. "When you think about it," Ian says, "the workplace is simply a collection of people trying to find meaning in their lives."

To illustrate how pervasive Ian's message is, consider this. In December of 2000, I met with two senior human resource people from a very large financial institution in Toronto. Their challenge was to identify a coach for the senior team. At one point the discussion shifted to how an organization can transform itself from what it is, to what it wants to become. I pointed out that unless everyone sees a "richly imagined future," transformation could not happen. One of the human resource people then asked me, "Do you know Ian Percy? I first heard that expression from him."

Named one of the top twenty-one speakers for the twenty-first century by *Successful Meetings* magazine, Ian Percy is a Certified Speaking Professional, or CSP, a designation held by fewer than 8% of professional speakers. He is also a member of the Canadian Speaking Hall of Fame. A psychologist with a column on performance improvement in Human Capital magazine, Ian has written a soul-stirring book on leadership entitled, *Going Deep*. His most recent book, *The Seven Secrets to a Life of Meaning*, shows people how to uncover their personal destinies. My feeling is that we will be seeing many more ripple effects of Ian's good work for decades to come. I am proud to call him my friend.

John Scherer is one of the most openly spiritual consultants I have ever met. Like Ian Percy, John has spoken in both the U.S. and Canadian offices of Aetna. Fully committed to the spiritual dimension in organizational development, he stressed that trust and interdependence must be created if an organization harbors the goal of becoming world class.

Working closely with the Aetna senior management team in Canada, John continually recommended that executives get in touch with their *center*. Recognizing their dependency on God and their responsibility for each other would, he believed, lead to excellence. That meant developing trust and recognizing and appreciating the interdependence of everyone working together. A coordinated team effort was essential. To make this happen, John demonstrated how the inner child in all of us strives to get out. He convinced us that we had to acknowledge this *being* to assure long-term success.

A turning point for the Aetna Canada team was a two-day confidence-building seminar. During one of the sessions, John asked the group if anyone wanted to share a private episode about his inner child. After a long silence Dobri Stojsic, the senior Vice President of Planning and Development, spoke up. Currently Dobri is the senior partner of "The Strategic Planning Group."

"I was a football star in high school but no matter how hard I tried I could never get my dad to attend one of the games. He was always too busy. Before the final game I went to him and asked, 'Dad, can you come to my game today?' He said, 'No son, I can't. You know I have work.'

"Well, I played my heart out and was selected as the most valuable player. But instead of feeling elated, I was terribly distraught because my father wasn't there to share this once-in-a-lifetime experience.

"When I got home I found my father was sitting on the sofa. He appeared somewhat inebriated. This threw me because my father did not drink. When I asked him what was wrong, he said, 'I decided to go to the game. Two young fellows sitting in front of me were cheering you on and I was so filled with pride I told them that you were my son. One of them said they were going to have a drink every time you made a good play and that they wanted me to join them. Please forgive me. I had no idea what a great football player you are.' Then the two of us started to cry and he grabbed me and hugged me tight."

By this time everyone in the room was teary-eyed. With that touching story, Dobri made a tremendous contribution. By sharing his story he bolstered trust. He opened the door for others to show the healing and connective power of the human spirit when the inner child in all of us is recognized.

Steve Solarz also made significant contributions. As I already mentioned, Steve was instrumental in introducing me to highly spiritual individuals in India. That wasn't the only place where I felt his impact. One day I was in New York with Steve and we were standing outside our hotel waiting for our prearranged ride. For whatever reason our driver did not show up. Suddenly a limo drove up and stopped. The driver rolled down the window on the passenger side and said, "Mr. Solarz, can I give you a lift?" Immediately, Steve said, "Yes. We are on our way to the airport; perhaps you could take us."

Once we were settled in the car, our driver introduced himself. "Mr. Solarz," he said, "I'm a recovering alcoholic. I haven't had a drink in ten years and there is something I need to say to you. You probably don't remember but I was part of your campaign team and distributed pamphlets when you were running for office. I must tell you that I only distributed half of them; the others I threw into a garbage can and then went off to a bar. I want to repair this with you. As part of the twelve-step program I had to say it."

Steve, magnanimous as well as generous, replied, "Thank you. It isn't necessary but I really appreciate it. You were a lot more supportive than a number of people who promised to distribute all of the pamphlets and then chucked them."

A spiritual incident like this one was a normal part of Steve's day. I was blessed to be a part of it.

LISTENING IS ONE THING, DOING IS ANOTHER

While the CEOs at Aetna brought in consultants and tried to follow their advice, by the mid-1990s most decisions were being made in the traditional way—at the top. There was an almost naïve belief that the Aetna world would continue without interruption and remain a powerhouse in the industry.

Beginning in 1995, the company embarked on a strategic review. Because it was decided that Aetna could not be *world class* in all of its businesses, a far-reaching decision evolved. The result of the review was to exit the property casualty business and use the proceeds of the sale to invest additional money to make Aetna the largest healthcare company in the United States.

Aetna, therefore, purchased U.S. Healthcare, paying over 8 billion dollars for it. This was followed with the acquisition of New York Healthcare. Some time later, Prudential Healthcare was acquired. Unfortunately, the hoped for economies did not materialize.

These actions were expected to recharge Aetna's financial batteries. Unfortunately, in my view, there was little evidence of the spiritual guidance that is so necessary during volatile times of turmoil and change that rocked the insurance and financial services business.

Melding Aetna and U.S. Healthcare operations was difficult. Many of the functions were kept separate and jobs were duplicated. When Aetna purchased New York Healthcare the redundancy increased. When Aetna bought Prudential Healthcare, the economies of scale escaped. There was little consolidation and not much attempt at finding out what all those affected employees felt about their situation. Unfortunately, in some cases these decisions were accompanied with a degree of arrogance and pride, and little if any appreciation for the fundamentals of integration.

After these purchases there seemed to be a lack of spiritual leadership. Involvement from the CEO of the day with the employee population was marginal at best. That meant that the people most immediately affected by policy—the employees—were not consulted. Their responsibility was limited to implementing the judgments handed down by senior management.

To me, one of the major tragedies that I witnessed within the organization was the unwillingness to engage the employee group in discussions about strategy and the future. It was, I feel, extremely insensitive. Not only were the minds of employees not addressed; the spirit bound up in their souls was deemed off-limits as well. Because of this dual deficiency, the full potential of the work force was not leveraged. And the problem didn't stop there. A more meaningful concern for the shareholders, customers, and suppliers was absent as well.

Interestingly, during these turbulent times there were people who continued their outstanding work in the community. Over time, however, this once proud sense of belonging to a caring family slowly eroded. How could it not, when the preoccupation of senior management was on the bottom line?

In yet another example of how businesses ignore their experienced employees and looked elsewhere for answers, Aetna appointed two CEOs with limited knowledge of the insurance business. These actions, I feel, cost Aetna the chance to be a better-focused and more successful organization.

I remember a classic example of not paying attention to the needs of others. The CEO was speaking at a formal dinner for 250 employees. Their peers had elected this group being celebrated as the most competent and focused customer service employees in the organization. The CEO gave a highly complimentary fifteen-minute speech and then excused himself because he had another engagement. That message of a quick exit spoke so loud it overcame all the praise he had given and left the audience deflated. This is not the way to either win hearts or promote loyalty.

The beginning of the end started when Aetna's leadership did not take the opportunity to bolster the company by helping employees to help themselves. When CEOs are driven by numbers and ignore historic values, replacing them with a mix of greed and personal ambition, only the worst can happen.

Personally, both guilt and sadness haunt me because I still do not fully understand why I did not speak up more forcefully when I saw what was happening. I think I sensed that once the decision was made to buy U.S. Healthcare, Aetna's future was already determined. My only excuse for not being more direct is that I concluded that, even as Chairman of Aetna International, my views were not terribly important to the CEO of the day. I had little contact with the U.S.-based businesses. And when I did, subjects like morale, productivity, and strategy implementation were seldom discussed.

Today the *new* Aetna is losing money, a situation that saddens me. After spending so many years at the company I still cheer it on, hoping for its success. Yet, I can't help say in hindsight that matters should have, and could have, been handled differently.

Despite all the turmoil that occurred during my last five years at Aetna and the irrevocable changes in the company that I loved, I found myself learning a whole new set of business lessons based on spirituality.

Given what happened to Aetna in the U.S., it isn't ironic to me that so many of my spiritual lessons were learned outside the country where Aetna experienced much success during those volatile years.

CHAPTER SEVEN:

Six Spiritual Lessons for Leaders

My last eight years at Aetna were centered on international business, an experience that profoundly changed my life. During that time I learned six simple lessons steeped in the spiritual underpinnings of the countries I traveled to and the people I met.

I truly believe that if these lessons were applied in the United States it could make significant and lasting positive changes in the business world. This is especially true as the traditional forms of business shift and change.

Change, of course, is constant and perhaps nowhere have such radical changes been seen as those that caused the rapid rise and equally quick crash of the dot.coms. One of the most crucial outgrowths of this event is the need to rely on and trust in something more durable than a hot career and an inflated sense of self-worth.

My personal fear is that these bright, young entrepreneurs may take after many of my generation and grasp onto a nearly religious belief in the *system in the organization*. In the lives of many with whom I worked, the company was their God, and all else—family, community, friends—was deemed less important. When this happened everyone involved lost out because there was no spiritual basis to living much less working.

I believe that being fully wrapped up in the perceived infinite power of the computer will garner the same outcome. Faith in technology is not the same as faith in a higher power.

My peers learned the hard way that no organization can promise lifetime employment, much less total fulfillment. The downsizing of corporate America, resulting in the loss of hundreds of thousands of jobs, left employees suffering both financially and personally. It takes this kind of jolt to show someone that he or she must look beyond a job for purpose in life.

It's time to learn new lessons that will make each person's career richer and more meaningful—lessons that can last a lifetime.

Six Lessons That Make a Difference

The six spiritual lessons I learned in my international dealings are:

1) patience
2) the power of silence
3) tasks versus relationships
4) the importance of meditation

5) the power of friendship
6) do your best and rely on the spirit of God for the result

Patience

A difficult virtue to develop, patience is not highly regarded in our society which expects instant gratification. This is not the case in most of the world, especially in Asia and Central and South America.

Here's an example. At a dinner in Washington, D.C., Ambassador Li Dayou, the Chinese Ambassador to the U.S., was enjoying his conversation with Senator Christopher Dodd. Toward the end of the evening, the Ambassador asked the Senator whether he had ever visited China. When Dodd told him that he had been to China the dialogue became even more animated. Eventually the topic shifted to post-graduate education and Ambassador Li mentioned that he had obtained his master's degree in Chinese history. Senator Dodd asked him how many years it took, and the Ambassador replied that he needed five years.

Surprised, the Senator told him that in his country it was possible to obtain such a degree in just two years.

The Ambassador paused and quietly told him that Chinese history goes back 5,000 years.

It takes patience to take the time to know a subject—and a person.

The Power of Silence

Many Westerners find silence almost oppressive. The next time you see a group of people at a gathering, watch how little effort there is to be silent. A pause in conversation is taken as an open invitation to drown out any possibility of quiet.

This is not the case in Asia. There silence is an important way to communicate. Often I think back to what was taught to me about the power of stillness from my Asian friends, especially Dr. Samuel Yin, our partner in the Aetna Taiwan venture, and Patrick Poon, Aetna's senior officer in Asia. Without talking, these men were very much at ease with others. Sam, for example, would sit and look at me for a few seconds before speaking. He was acknowledging my presence without saying a word and by doing so put his mind and spirit at peace.

Sometimes, silence is worth a thousand words.

Tasks Versus Relationships

Western culture is task-oriented. If you need proof, just look at how our business schools train their students. With surgical precision, men and women are taught to identify problems, evaluate risks, apply remedies, then move on to the next challenge.

In contrast, in South America and Asia, as well as emerging nations, much more emphasis is placed on relationship building for very solid reasons. Friendship, confidence, interdependence, and trust are the potential outcomes of building relationships. Asians, for instance, are confident that tasks will be resolved successfully, and in a mutually-beneficial way, once camaraderie is established and maintained.

My own experience in Asia bore this out. It took time, but finally I began to understand that our Asian colleagues were trying to impart the strength and wisdom of building relationships when I thought they were dragging their feet. I've had the good fortune to be taught by many wonderful Asians who brought home to me how important it is to forge relationships in order to effectively deal with critical business issues. Friends rather than strangers can achieve more, and where logic fails, friendship can survive. The bonds of friendship tap into the spirit, where deep connections are made.

I experienced this first-hand with Dr. Samuel Yin when plans for Aetna's expansion extended beyond Taiwan. As our partner in Taiwan, he had worked hard in supporting our efforts to secure a license for China. He felt that when that happened, his share should be 35% of Aetna's share, instead of the 20% we thought was equitable.

His people and our staff had tried to resolve their differences over nearly six months with no success. With timing becoming critical, both teams suggested that Sam and I sit down for a final evaluation and—everyone hoped—a possible breakthrough.

We tried, but well past midnight it was clear that a solution was evading us. Finally in desperation I said, "Sam, will you be meditating tomorrow morning?"

"Of course," he replied, "just as I do every morning."

"Then I have a request. Tomorrow, would you please think of the needs of your friend?"

Standing, a gesture that meant that our meeting was over, Sam nodded.

The next morning at six Sam phoned me and asked me to join him in his suite. Once I got there, he greeted me in silence and motioned for me to sit as he did so himself. And there we sat for about five minutes, just looking at each other.

Then, with a soft voice, Sam said, "While I was meditating I thought of the needs of my friend. I want to accommodate him." Then he did something that shocked me. He got up, walked over to me, and embraced me. This was astounding, as public displays of affection are not common in China.

Standing straight, he continued. "Leave the announcement to me. I will notify my people that the issue has been resolved in a way to support my friend."

Enormously relieved and touched, I told him, "Thank you, Sam. I am in your debt."

Later that day I asked Patrick Poon about the meaning of Sam's hug. He told me, "He now considers you as part of his extended family and expects that you will conduct yourself accordingly."

Another episode showed me the power of relationship versus task resolution. By the time I was chairman, a certain decision regarding Taiwan was made without consulting Sam. It wasn't done with intended malice; sadly, it was just another example of western insensitivity.

Within a few hours I heard that Sam was embarrassed—he felt he had lost face by being excluded—and very upset with Aetna. As it happened I was on my way to Taiwan and, disembarking from the plane, I expected to see the Rolls Royce that Sam always sent waiting to take me to my hotel. In its place, was a company car. Obviously, there was a problem.

When we arrived at Sam's office, Sam greeted my team and me with politeness. After the meeting, however, he asked me to remain for a few minutes.

He came right to the point. "Is this the way we treat family?" he asked. With this one forthright question Sam reduced the business issues to the spiritual dimension of our relationship.

"No, it's not," I admitted. "I apologize and feel terrible that it happened. I'm really sorry."

Sam nodded his acceptance of my apology and I knew in that moment that forgiveness was a by-product of spirituality at work.

Building relationships is the most efficient and meaningful way to accomplish tasks.

The Importance of Meditation

As I've mentioned throughout this book, meditation, for me, has been a life-altering habit. It has changed my existence and made it more fulfilling, both personally and professionally.

But I didn't fully appreciate the power of meditation until I did business in Asia and South America. In various countries I experienced first-hand how meditation separates the eternal from the mundane. The *centering* it offers allows you to be in touch with your soul and connect with others. Meditation calms the mind and cheers the heart and most of all, fixes the soul in the hands of the Creator. Then you can carry out the divine message of doing what is right. I feel strongly that meditation has the therapeutic power to fix—and cure—our fractured world.

The answers to problems, including ones in business, are inside us.

The Power of Friendship

Recently, I received a wonderful gift from Aetna's chief representatives in China. These are the management people from various cities throughout the country where Aetna hopes to secure insurance licenses as these markets are opened up to foreign competition. The present was a scroll created by a Beijing artist. In Chinese characters, it states, *San Gao Shui Chang.* This expression means, "Your contribution is as high as a mountain, your reputation will last as long as a river." What a spiritually-infused sentiment from true friends!

For me, friendship is the spiritual relationship that exists between two people. Bea, my wife, is my closest friend. The love and friendship we share has grown over the forty-plus years we've been together. And even though we don't see many of our Aetna-extended family both here and abroad often enough, we know that the friendships we forged continue to bridge distances.

Love is a gift of the spirit, and friendship is the expression of that love. In international business, I've seen how the enormous power of friendship during times of crisis, misunderstanding, and stress was able to resolve problems with honor and grace.

Without friendship in business, no endeavor will truly succeed.

Do Your Best and Rely on the Spirit of God for the Result

Doing your best requires one constant: living in the present. The baggage of the past coupled with the anticipation of future problems saps both energy and creativity. Lose focus and your efforts will suffer. This is especially true in negotiations. Worrying about the future or what might happen handicaps a successful resolution.

That's why this lesson includes the previous five. Living in the present is easier to achieve through meditation, which leads you to live in the moment. Meditation requires patience and silence, and shows the way to understanding that building relationships is all-important. Once that bond is forged, the power of friendship can see you through trying times.

Time after time, my experiences in China bore this out. Consider that I traveled to China every two or three months for five years to meet with various government agencies and senior regulators to secure a license.

Each time upon my return, my colleagues in Hartford would tease me asking, "Do we have a license yet?"

"No, not yet," I would answer.

"When will we get the license?" they would press.

"Soon," I'd say.

"And when is soon?" they'd want to know.

"In a country with 5,000 years of history, soon could be twenty years."

Of course getting the license didn't take twenty years. The business return for living this lesson and all that it contains, is success. But much more than financial return, living life by and through these lessons can provide a deeper meaning to each day. It means greeting each morning with thanks for the blessing of being alive.

Be the best you can be. The rest is in the hands of the Creator.

CHAPTER EIGHT:

A Call for Corporate Spiritual Leadership

Where do we go from here?

In this volatile age of rapid-fire technologies, more and more reliance on things rather than people, and the quest for ever-widening bottom lines, what is today's CEO to do? Executive groups calling for strategy sessions with the hope of finding the magic bullet that will bring success are exercises in futility. If organizations are led today as they were even five years ago, I believe there is a pretty good chance that when adversity hits, failure will follow.

So the answer is change, a mutable situation that strikes fear into many and for good reason. The world has witnessed more change in the past fifty years than in the previous five hundred. In the time of our grandparents and parents, change was gradual and, to some extent, predictable. However, in our day the speed of change has been increasing almost geometrically; dealing with that change is one of the most challenging and constant issues that humans face.

In business too the changes have been swift. The industrial age was replaced by the information age. Currently, we live in the era of e-commerce and Internet access spreads by the minute. Markets have shifted from local to regional to national to global. Along with these adaptations the traditional organizational business structure changed too, shifting from pyramidal to flat.

In the pyramidal structure, information was gathered and passed up the chain of command until it reached the top where the CEO was located. With access to all the accumulated information, he would make a decision and then pass it down the line for implementation. Employees knew only pieces of what was going on. This military-style model was used for centuries.

Today the flat organizational structure has taken hold. Because of technological advances, most employees have access to the same information the CEO has. This circumstance can powerfully influence responsibility and accountability because workers can act on the information. Young employees see their careers as opportunities to self-actualize. They have neither trust nor confidence in an organization to protect them, much less offer them lifetime employment. Instead, they rely on their own expertise and competence and take full responsibility for their careers.

And something even newer is happening right now. In the past ten years a brand-new economy, e-commerce, has emerged.

This revolutionary economy is volatile. While it shows great promise it is already incurring significant problems. Nonetheless, this newcomer has made a big impact on how the economic world market will evolve over the next few years. For one thing, young, bright entrepreneurs are chucking or totally avoiding the established way of getting ahead in large, relatively stable organizations. Instead, they develop e-based enterprises and then sell them quickly for often great profit. Even with the recent free-fall of the dot-coms, e-commerce is not going to disappear. Indeed, at some future point I think we will see the convergence of the new and old economies. In this melded business environment, each one will, I expect, share lessons and complement each other in the global marketplace in order to survive and prosper.

THE NEW AGE LEADER

With all this upheaval there is a priceless opportunity to make a really powerful change and practice business with a spiritual basis. In the 21st century, the notion of leadership based on control and command won't work successfully any more. Rather, it's time for the New Age leader to emerge. This person must turn over power to his or her employees. By doing so, he or she will lock in a competitive advantage in the global marketplace for a fundamental reason. Their employees, who will feel honored and appreciated, will give their best.

The New Age leader, therefore, needs to be someone whose expertise and competency are world class, and who practices the very same changes as that of the evolving organization. This person will embrace the role of **servant**, **shepherd** and **steward**.

- As a **servant**, the New Age leader knows that part of the basic responsibility is to serve employees, shareholders, and customers alike. All these people share a stake in the company's success.

- As a **shepherd**, the New Age leader must have an extra commitment and concern for the entire company and literally watch over it.

- As a **steward**, the performance of the New Age leader must be judged by the company's financial performance. His or her legacy must be a prime focus of what to do to accomplish this objective while respecting the other two roles.

Six Traits of the New Age Leader

1) The New Age leader is a mentor and coach. Teaching is part of the job, which creates a positive environment.

2) The New Age leader is a visionary. This leader is able to visualize his or her business running at peak level. Not only that, this leader must have the ability to look into the future and interpret the changes underway in the marketplace, the product line, and the general direction of the economy.

3) The New Age leader is generous. He or she doesn't take credit for all that goes right or blame subordinates for all that goes wrong. On the contrary, the New Age leader shares successes and understands failure. Giving praise when it's earned and credit when it is due, are the real and effective hallmarks of this person.

4) The New Age leader is participative. Available to listen and to be fully active in all aspects of his or her business, this leader creates an all-inclusive environment felt by every employee.

5) The New Age leader is inspirational. Breathing life into an organization, this person motivates people to perform at their highest levels because they are free to tap into and use their most creative talent, self-expression, and energy. Because of this, employees feel honored and in response take on both responsibility and accountability.

6) The New Age leader is strategic. While personal characteristics and attributes got this person his or her job, they do not assure success. Learning new skills and rigorously challenging the status quo are critical because they lead to creating new strategies and successfully implementing them.

New Age leadership, therefore, can't be anything *but* spiritual. The New Age leader, by tapping into the spiritual source within, can then:

- Overcome the fear of appearing weak or indecisive by bravely showing what he or she is really made of

- Admit limitations and therefore welcome the help of all employees

- Deal with ambiguity and uncertainty with a lot more ease

THE NEW AGE DIFFERENCE

The behavior of the New Age leader, therefore, is in direct contrast to corporate America's ongoing commitment to endlessly reorganize in order to eliminate waste and duplication. When this happens, the company is reconfigured yet again. Experts are consulted, charts are presented, some belts are tightened (but not often at the top), and in the process any spiritual life that existed is squeezed out leaving a dry husk of an organization full of apprehensive employees. Is this the formula for ongoing success? I think not.

While the current buzzwords are *organizational transformation*, I question whether the term is more innovative than the actual policy. To me, transformation should be rooted in a strategic vision of markets, customers, employees, and shareholders. To do that, organizational transformation does not take place until and unless there is personal transformation at the top.

That means that leaders must tap into their own best selves in order to bring out the best in others. When this happens, when a spiritual link is forged between people, then success will follow. And in down times, a solid basis for support and rebuilding will exist to make success happen once again.

I've talked about a number of New Age leaders who made a lasting impression on me with their instinctive use of spirituality. Each practiced the role of servant, shepherd, and steward. Here are a few others I will never forget.

Federico Reyes

Federico Reyes was the second CEO of the joint venture between Aetna and its Mexican partner Bancomer. He negotiated a tough partnership arrangement and our people felt that he was demanding, and that he paid a lot of attention to details. Of course he did, because during the discussions he represented the Bancomer interests. As a steward, he was caretaker of Bancomer's concerns until the deal was done. As a shepherd, he had responsibility to both parties to make certain the joint venture succeeded and that their interests were safeguarded. As a servant, he put the interests of his company first.

Once the deal was done and he was appointed the CEO of the joint venture, his responsibility shifted; now he represented the interests of both partners. He went to great lengths to consult with us well in advance of any significant change in direction.

His role didn't stop there because his person-to-person influence permeated the office. Walking through the various work areas of the company was a delightful experience. It was a very friendly environment where big smiles and waves to visitors were the norm. And that was Federico's doing. He worked hard and allowed his team great latitude to improve results.

I remember a dinner with Federico after he had moved up within the Bancomer Group. His heart was still with Seguros Monterrey Aetna and he truly missed the people he had worked with so closely. These are the hallmarks of a leader who fully understands and supports the spiritual component of business. That's why, to me, he will always stand out as a special leader. And he wasn't an exception in Mexico. His actions were more typical of the quality of senior business leaders I met.

Gonzalo de la Puente y Lavalle

Gonzalo de la Puente y Lavalle became chairman of our joint venture company Wiese Aetna Compania de Seguros in Peru. Articulate and open, he wielded power with caution. At the same time, he extended himself in such a way that visiting him felt like seeing an old friend. It takes a special talent to meet a stranger and within an hour start building a relationship, but that's what he did at our first meeting. This was in sharp contrast to those of us trained in the *my cynicism is a shield for self-preservation* school of business. Indeed, both Pancho Wiese and Augusto Wiese, whose Bank Wiese was our partner in Peru, exuded the same spiritual characteristics that indicated their perception of their role as business leaders representing the interests of their country.

And the spiritual dimension didn't stop with that generation. Gonzalo's daughter, Caridad de la Puente, was a remarkable young executive. Her wisdom and prudence were never sacrificed while she made the tough management decisions required in the competitive financial service business. Her extended family shared a common belief on how business leaders must shoulder the additional responsibility of protecting and improving the marketplace to better serve all the citizens.

Gustavo Marturet

Gustavo Marturet, chairman of Banco Mercantil in Venezuela, and chairman of our joint venture in Venezuela, was the same way. Like many other leaders in the Americas, Gustavo's responsibilities in no way conflicted with his judgment about fair play and flexibility.

The aura of spirituality that surrounded him was both attractive and inviting. When Gustavo heard that my friend, Ian Percy, had asked me to contribute a chapter to *Going Deep,* his very successful book on spirituality, he requested a copy to read and share with his associates.

A deeply religious person, during one of his visits to Hartford he expressed the desire to attend mass at St. Joseph's Cathedral. It was a delight to see a business leader act in this way. With all the attention that high-level business people in this country get, how often do they reveal their spiritual roots? Religious beliefs, of course, are a private matter, but showing one's spiritual core is not.

Patrick Poon

Patrick Poon, understands this as well. The aforementioned Patrick, one of the most accomplished insurance executives in Asia, was country manager in Taiwan where he started Aetna's operations. He assumed additional responsibilities for Hong Kong and Greater China as the Senior Vice President for Greater China, a position he held until Aetna sold its international operations to ING. He continues his executive responsibility for ING.

Patrick wrote a book entitled, *Be Bold,* which became a bestseller in Taiwan. In it he describes his management and leadership philosophy. Knowing him, it's easy to see where his views come from.

He speaks softly, seldom raising his voice. Repeatedly he has created an environment where the management team and all employees strive for excellence. A careful risk-taker, he constantly allows people to make mistakes as long as those mistakes are not repeated and that something worthwhile is gained from the experience. His trust in people pays off. When I asked him a short time ago to describe his management style, he replied, "Technology and service." State-of-the-art technology has kept his operations at the cutting edge above most competitors. Service to the customers is a sacred trust that permeates his organization. Ultimately, he credits his people for world-class performance.

Recently Aetna Taiwan was recognized as "the most friendly customer service company" in the country by

Modern Insurance Magazine, a well-known industry publication in Taiwan.

Patrick's standard which drives the company, shone through on September 21, 1999, when Nantou, the central area of Taiwan, suffered a severe earthquake. Within hours, the people of Aetna Taiwan organized truckloads of supplies, food, and medicine that were dispatched to the scene.

*   *   *   *   *

Servant. Shepherd. Steward. Each of the people listed above understands what it means to be servant, shepherd and steward, and practices it. Without a spiritual basis in their lives they would not be able to fulfill the three roles, and they would not have accomplished all they have done so far.

They accepted their leadership roles with a passion for results but not at the expense of their values. I am proud to know them.

EPILOGUE

Today's Response to Tomorrow's Call

After my retirement from Aetna in 2000, I met with my close friend and adviser Eric Barton, now Chairman of Miller Dallas, a relocation counseling company that coaches senior executives how to re-enter the business world, to talk about my future. Eric was a natural choice. A deeply religious man, Eric's spirituality shines through everything he does. His success in the relocation counseling business can be traced to his great understanding and concern for those who suffer and are in pain. His empathy with people who lose their jobs is legendary.

During that meeting I asked Eric for help in sorting out what kinds of activities should occupy the next part of my life. In response, he requested a list with the names of people with whom I worked and lived. He wanted to interview them to get a fix on how I was perceived.

After his interviews, he gave me a summary. Once again, I witnessed the essence of friendship. The people who spoke to Eric—some of them were independent contractors who consulted with Aetna—told him about the relationships they shared with me. They spoke about how, intuitively, they knew they were respected not only for the work they did but also for their individual selves. This was one of the most satisfying *reviews* I have ever received in my career. When I asked Eric what to do next, his advice was simple. "Write what you have learned and pass it on to others," he told me. "Speak to them and mentor them. Make sure that spiritual link stays alive every day."

Eric Barton has set a standard that every chairman could learn from—he keeps showing me new spiritual paths. For instance, over the years both Eric and his late wife, Ruth, were solidly committed to helping the less fortunate. They were involved in many outreach programs in Toronto. Then one day Eric announced that he was going to Calcutta for three months to lend a hand in a hospital managed by Mother Theresa's order. Having seen the inspirational nun on one of her Canadian visits, he was so struck by her saintliness and life's mission that he longed to be part of it.

As impressed as I was by his commitment, I didn't fully understand the spirit that was moving him. When I asked him why he just didn't send money, he replied, "That won't do it. My soul needs to witness and feel the suffering. I need to help lighten the pain and the sorrow."

This extraordinary sacrifice became a pattern in his life. Every two or three years he would take a leave of absence and travel to places like Haiti and offer what he could to the terminally ill, the destitute, and the downtrodden.

Eric's spiritual journeys are closer to home as well. He supports the Yonge Street Mission in Toronto, an excellent organization focused on aiding young homeless people to redirect their lives. Every year he writes hundreds of letters to associates throughout Canada asking for funds for this extremely worthy cause.

His alumni of senior executives have been profoundly impacted, as have I, by his personality, his commitment to doing good, and his great love of God. With his generous spirit he directs his whole being to encourage, guide, and support others. It is no exaggeration to say that Eric Barton is a modern-day saint at work.

WHERE TO GO FROM HERE?

Helped enormously by the far journeys I have taken in business, I've discovered a few things about myself in particular and life in general.

I've found that with all the differences that exist between people, there is one constant: spirituality is the common link we share. It bonds us as brothers and sisters in the human family. It permits us to see the face of God in each other.

In business, the power of the spirit can lead to solutions based on friendship and trust—the best, most effective way to solve problems. To make this work, a leader must be honest and open with his spiritual connections. Too many leaders mouth words of love and partnership while practicing a regime based on fear and hatred.

Yet the spirit seems to be directing itself toward companies through receptive individuals. These accessible men and women are the ones who will achieve great success. Not only will they create an atmosphere where the best of employees are recognized and nurtured, inspiring them to excel; they will create a legacy that will support and propel their companies and organizations into the future. Everyone touched by the spirit will live each day fully, engaged with others and aware of the moment.

Businesses already contain the greatest assets possible: the people within them. With leaders who serve, who understand their role and what they can do to bring about positive changes in themselves and the people around them, one thing is clear:

They will discover the hidden success factor in business: spirituality.

* * * * *

When the spirit is honored, there is little possibility of failure or disappointment.

About the Author

Michael A. Stephen dedicated his executive leadership to creating positive business environments where managers and employees could experience individual and personal transformation. This, he knew, was the ultimate secret to assuring profitable organizational growth and development.

A Doctor of Letters, honoris casua, Mike was Chairman of Aetna International, Inc. when he retired in 2000, after twenty-six years with the company.

Under his leadership, Aetna entered the newly emerging markets of Argentina, Peru, Indonesia and China while expanding its insurance lines in New Zealand and Chile. Representative offices were established in Beijing and Shanghai in preparation for entering the insurance business in China. Michael led this initiative and built relationships with the senior decision-makers in China. In 1997, after overcoming great odds, Aetna became only the second U.S. company to be granted approval for a life insurance license in China.

While achieving this incredible feat, Mike continued to provide remarkable leadership of Aetna's interests with the regulators and senior government officials in Asia, Central and South America.

Meditation and developing his spiritual awareness continues to be part of his daily life. In addition, to an active consulting practice, Michael is often sought as a corporate speaker on the moral and bottom-line value of combining business and spirituality.

The parents of four and grandparents of six, he and his wife Beatrice live in Toronto, Canada.

Have Michael Stephen speak
to your organization!

Please send inquiries to:

Lynn Hellinger

LRHellinger@aol.com